ICE, MOUTH, SONG

D1593214

ICE, MOUTH, SONG

A Collection of Poems

Rachel Contreni Flynn

TUPELO PRESS
Dorset, Vermont

Ice, Mouth, Song
Copyright © 2005 by Rachel Contreni Flynn

ISBN-10   1-932195-18-1
ISBN-13   978-1-932195-18-7
Printed in Canada

Library of Congress Control Number:
2003114634
First paperback edition, May 2005

Tupelo Press
PO Box 539, Dorset, Vermont 05251
802.366.8185   Fax 802.362.1883
editor@tupelopress.org   web www.tupelopress.org

Cover & text design by Howard Klein

For Patrick Flynn
...who is my chiefest comforter on earth...
Anne Bradstreet

CONTENTS

THREE

FINE

Find the rip cord,
find the trapdoor,
find the child

in a snowbank
singing
the old song:

We are dying
of the cold and not
of the dark...

In the lake
there's an inch
between frozen

and not yet.
There's a face
pressed there,

doing fine.

The mouth practices
kisses all winter,
turning purple.

This is childhood
in three pieces:
ice, mouth, song...

This is bone china
buried in the yard.

A plate held
to the sun shows
a hand behind it—

brushing dirt away
or waving.

ONE

The Match Girl Lights Them One By One

I must not envy sparrows.

I must not punish my body.

I must not pull the wings off.

I must not disinfect everything.

I must not shrivel into dust mites.

I must not dream inside a chimney.

I must not seek comfort from this.

DEAD CENTER

August in Indiana:

a heavy moon hung over space
where there was almost nothing

but one big town at dead center.

Grasshoppers popped under tires,
the trees swelled with grackles,

and I amused myself with windmills—
the solitary geometry of glint and spin,

slowing then standing motionless
until the sky raised its dark fist.

The autumn my mother left
a coldness opened...

Beans dried to snakes' tails in the fields,
and my chest filled with rust.

In the snow I walked the pastures

in an orange poncho
my father could see from the house.

Once I told him to stop waving at me.

Once I said *Maybe I'll just keep walking.*

And once I slid the poncho
to the near-frozen middle of Moots Pond

just to watch him run from the house
barefoot and wild.

STONE FRUIT

for Judith

1.

At the edge of the woods,
my sister snacks on day lilies

while I pry a doll's head
from the hole in a locust tree.

Reaching through the neck,
I pull wet stuff that fills

the eyes with illness—

a nest of milkweed silks
and four dead voles.

My sister's mouth gleams
with pollen,

and when I show her the voles,
she smiles a brief, vivid arc.

2.

The mobile
looming

over me:

spinning shapes
of pastries.

My sister scaling
the crib,

gripping

the rail,
a wedge of cake

passing.

Three hands
reaching.

3.

The confusion began in Paris

when the black-haired lady
selling horse steaks
befriended our mother

> (who carried us
> in slings through the market
> and said she needed better meat
> for her babies)

What babies? the lady crooned,
thrusting taped parcels across the bloody table,

those are apricots in a sack—
you know the apricot—

the stone fruit from the family of roses?

4.

We cooked

for ourselves
late at night: fry-bread

in a black skillet.
It took both of us

to lift the pan
and pour hot lard

down the sink's
cool throat.

We ate

quickly: bannock
hard as gravel

and marmalade
from a cold pot—

furtive as rodents
in the red brick kitchen—

then we scrubbed steel wool
across our mouths.

We pinched

blue fish waving
under the burners

and filled ourselves
with sleep.

RED BRICK HUNGRY

for Maureen

The house fell out of the woods full-grown,
and we moved in, removing

the plastic fountain of angels bubbling,
pudgy in the foyer.

Squirrels in the brick walls all winter,
corn smut on the screens in late summer,

and the baby sick for months—
yellow and thin—our father weeping,

all of us bending
in that impossible shadow.

♦♦♦

I am loyal to my gut
which is a red brick, hungry

for more mud and sun,
which is to say,

lonely.

♦♦♦

The pale knife
of a mantis clings

to the precise wall of our house.
It tries to stay cool, do some good,

or just keep quiet.

♦♦♦

The baby lives.

I prop her against
the headboard to read

how Laura Ingalls twists hay
in the barn with Pa,

Louis Barnavelt solves the mystery
of the clock in the walls,

and Anne of Green Gables
saves everyone.

♦♦♦

When no one is looking,

I feed her
bits of cupcake

bought with money stolen
from our father's wallet.

Still, she sleeps too much.
Her butternut skin alarms me

into not looking.

♦♦♦

One summer
a truck pulls up
and drives off

with all
the little things:

books and silver,
linens, dishes,

brother, sister.

♦♦♦

Then
I'm loyal
to the salt lick
in the woods
dwindling
by rain
and tongue
and time.

At dark, it shrieks white
as a crazy woman's nightdress.

♦♦♦

Res ipsa loquitor: The thing speaks for itself.
I will grow to study justice. The thorn of myself,
the thing in the foot. I will rent air in old rooms
and curl against the wall, drunk. Some knife.

♦♦♦

I was in love

with the World Book, proud of chimneys
in pictures of Dresden and London—

rubble and the survivors—

the towns full of middle fingers,
up-raised

and still red.

♦♦♦

I'm baking
shortbread,

each a brick
drained of red.

The fork
makes rows
of holes.

I name them:
brother, sister. Brother, sister.

♦♦♦

In Chicago red brick
is everywhere and car alarms,
broken bottles, ice.

I call my sister to ask
the names of shells and insects
and if she remembers

the quiet of the woods at night.

I read by flashlight,
she slept with fingers
in her mouth.

♦♦♦

I learn many things
        in law school:

the elements

of bad faith, anti-trust,
        and trespassing.

How to estimate
punitive damages.

But mostly

that the liquid form of brick
            is not blood

            but jug wine.

            ♦♦♦

I live in old buildings
with old women who show me

their paper doll arms. I tell them
pigeons sit on the window unit

and fill my room with low sounds—
a terrible loudness of sleeping too much.

            ♦♦♦

One summer
a truck pulls up

and dumps
a load of bricks in the alley.

They stay.

I'm afraid
when it snows:

the bricks covered over
show red in spots

like a pile of bodies, shot.

DAUGHTERS

Our father skipped
the flat stone of himself

across the marsh one morning,

and the water frothed
with fish in pursuit,

birds dove from trees,
and beasts sprang

from the woods—

ears back, teeth bared,
sleek with hunger.

Even the sun bolted up
and cast her huge hand frantic

into the marsh
to be the one

to find him.

Heat Rising

The stink of something newly dead seeps
from the wood box, but instead of touching

the bloat and worms and floppy neck, the brothers
break themselves apart to burn, and the sisters sneak

to the attic to outwit the cold. They curl
around the chimney until their hair turns to smoke,

their eyes to ash. Come spring, the mother
spreads buckets of her children on the garden

where she spends long days in sweet air,
crawling backwards through the dirt,

nursing on hard green starts of strawberries.

Rolling

Forces shall appear and profane the temple and fortress...
    And they shall set up the abomination that makes desolate.
                Daniel 11:31

We're smoking the Bible
page by page

in the abandoned bomb shelter
while above us

God sent his angel and shut the lions' mouths

alfalfa sobs in the sun.
Every so often,

a train passes...

And I fell on my face in a deep sleep.

My brother's silence
is silence. He's no longer blonde

but buzz cut, and the walls
tremble with a train.

Back home

the God in whose hand is your breath

our father ages in the wingback,
and our sister grows thin...

and the wind carried them away
and not a trace could be found.

Dirt falls on us
in the cloud of us: we're rolling—

we're smoking our names
that lodge in our lungs

and a stone was brought
and laid upon the mouth of the den

until we choke and hack
like chopping sumac in a ditch.

We're rolling
in the noise of it: coughing,

concrete falling, rolling
in a cavity of mice and grubs

for it was broken
and the sanctuary trampled

and not speaking and not leaving—
just rolling.

LIMOGES

Midnights, I meet
my dead grandmother
under the broken magnolia

where she's prepared
a tea caddy of Pall Malls
and little pills.

She waits for me
to sit properly, lick my lips,
ask for a hit.

How many daughters, I say,
will it take? Her earrings
are stained bells, her hands

a tangled lapful of cancer,
and she clutches the teapot
to her fine blouse.

The Limoges explodes.

I gather shards like pink leaves
from the cold dirt, willingly.
Oh, have some class,

she scolds. *Get up and have a glass
of sherry,* and she passes me
how many mouths full

of syrup-fire? How many
biscuits of Demerol—
how many daughters?

My grandmother burns a long hole
in the upholstery. She's going,
saying only, *Goodnight girl*

of my stature, my sack
of belly. . . Goodnight little girl
whose name ends in hell.

PEPPERCORN

A little bit

        makes it right—

To lease a room over the kitchen,
the servant trades a peppercorn:

        hard nothing,
        bitter lump,
        sufficient

consideration. Consider—

small is better though

        it doesn't matter—

and the year my sister shrank
into a stalk of goldenrod:

        dry reed,
        crisp swaying,
        thin

snapping-off. She speckled the fields
behind our father's house

with a helpless nodding. Hard nothing.
Pittance. *Pretty little*
        grass girl.

Once I dreamed I picked and clipped her

into a centerpiece and set a table:

      utensils, crystal,
      roast and new
      potatoes,

the lovely yellow bouquet.

      And we were praised.

BLACK FELT

Who are you arriving
in the bloody dress
with a gourd in your hands,

and why do you hollow
the gourd into a birdhouse?
You tack strips of black felt

to my back, saying *Fly away.*
But I'm tired, and it's nice
in the gourd, smooth and dark—

the small room you made me.
Through the hole I see
almost nothing

but once in a while a flutter
of you in your dress, sewing claws
onto others in the house.

THE PERIL OF GOOSEBERRIES

The first lesson is to cut them open—
that way, a light syrup. Otherwise,
bitter raisins.

I make preserves
as if stocking a bomb shelter,
as if I could starve

any minute. I have my reasons:
the lids boiling, that music, the risk
of scalding, the wax puck,

hardening. It's the idea of danger
and containment, the cool press
of the basement, and the urgency

of standing in the dark
with hot jars in my arms.
It makes me think of fire

in a submarine: that air, that screaming,
and the sub revealing
nothing—just a cool oval, loitering—

until the slow rise to the surface
and the lucky survivor
blinking in the light.

Sleep

I sleep the smell of bricks and books,
the shucking of corn,
the porch swing on fire.

I sleep the wake of my mother's red thresher.

I sleep the business of gray cranes,
angry cats, bear pits.
In Belize, 90 degrees—I sleep a manatee mother
at the mouth of Monkey River—

I poke her with a stick.

I'm sick in my sleep—a curl of caulk in the sheets—
I sleep mercury, tarot cards, ginger ale.
Over again, I sleep

lavender, camphor, hands.
(Her yellow dress full of strawberries? I sleep them.)

And fog.
Fieldstones and gunshots—
a face over the flashlight, saying *Cold*
is the size of loneliness.

I sleep the front yard in her robe, waiting.

I sleep buckeyes and money—
gibberish and Jesus—
a brittle board over the cistern,
there I sleep jump-roping.

Falling. Algae. I sleep well
and metal pail—a dark circle, a pit
of lavender, camphor, hands—

in her robe
in the yard, waiting... I sleep my fist

and raise myself, shaking.

Two

CORAL

Because it wards off the evil eye,
I built a house of it—crusty pink, oceanic—
half-stone, half-flesh.

And I was happy in it

just deer coming
to rub and lick, only birds roosting
in the spurs.

All day light came through,
diffuse…air too, private and cool
as a lagoon.

Plants grew.

I stacked old ink sketches
in the attic to make room for wide canvases,
and started painting mangroves,

swags of kelp,
shelves of rock lit hydra-bright.
Then the boat of night

scraped up:

Oh you. You
with your pirate's patch
and pick axe.

STATE HOME, 1984

Wiping down old people,
I think of nothing living:

cardboard, pine pulp, concrete.

No, I think of hurting myself—

for the chance to lie down,
for the softness of gauze.

The gowns are countless
blue stars. I untie them,

and the vest restraints.

I'm fifteen and afraid
of their breath in my hair.

A man dies in the tub.
I rinse him off, then

go for help.

The nights are a spray
against a tub of spit trays.

I hoard my paychecks.

There is no help. I lift him
to standing against me,

to slow dancing,

to pivoting
into a smooth, vinyl chair.

If I were in the hospital,
think of the smoothness.

Think how breakfast would come—
the breast of half a grapefruit,

its happy eye.

GOLD STARS

It was forbidden to touch
the Hummels in my aunt's pretty house,
arranged just so and shut
in the glass cabinet, pigeon-toed,
rosy-faced, holding kittens or balloons,
their porcelain bellies bulging
under pinafores and overalls...

and it was wrong to kiss
the high school janitor after track practice
against a concrete wall
in the band room vestibule
where a fake velvet blanket draped
the old upright piano,
and a long row of trombones tilted
in their shiny black cases...

but these
were the gold stars I gave myself
when I thought no one was watching
and nothing would get broken,
and I was brilliant: easing

the little brass latches
and reaching in.

BILLBOARD, IOWA

Welcome to the land of 60-foot buffets
and towns that grunt: Stout, Galt, Otho.

Feel free to stop, breathe deep, buy pumpkins,
but don't think that's a red bandana

dropped in a harvested field—it's what's left
of a fox, snagged by a rotating auger.

And don't go near the tree houses—
the underbrush is rigged with spring guns

and full of malicious pigs. We shoot
old basketballs here and toss them in the creek

where they bleach into a hundred milky eyes.
We sit on porches and sofas waiting

for the bug zapper to sizzle on, thinking
of claw foot tubs and how we set razor blades

flat on the water to float. From time to time
boys in trucks drive through town beating

the mailboxes with 2x4s. We go to bed late,
and every night marigolds detonate our brains.

THE PHYSICS OF THE INEVITABLE

My hometown mourns the farm boy
who kicked a cob stuck
in the combine's flywheel,
and I imagine his foot swinging just as he was thinking
    I know better than this,
but it was too great, the weight
of his crusted boot,
not to follow through.
    And I think

of the Viking ship pitching
in its greasy groove all summer
at Lake Schaefer, and how the carny said
It don't hardly take any juice at all to run this ride—
once set to rock, it just about
    went on its own.

And I've made love like this,
the whole time thinking
    how I wasn't,
the whole time my mind watching my body
as a thing in motion but not a mystery,
more like math—more like the arc of a burlap sack
tossed from Moots Creek Bridge,
then the heavy spiral
    of rocks and cats.

NERVE GAS WAREHOUSE

Around it, the midwestern woods
do as they're told: moderate growth,

light leaves. No dense underbrush,
no large noisemakers, though turkeys

sometimes stroll near the gates,
and a small brook floods its banks

with each heavy rain. The guards
spit seeds and make calls to home

while behind steel doors, the nerve gas
swirls in boxed tubes. All day

the temperature regulates. At dusk,
deer with well-hidden zippers advance.

Birds of Paradise

On the 96th floor
of the Hancock,
       you're amazed at the view,

but you must be subdued, as flawless
as flatware in your
       angular haircut, as bright as the glare

of chandelier against wineglass against Plexiglas.
An Allstate exec
       in monogrammed cuffs

says *This high up the windows flex,*
they're synthetic. But he has
       such big teeth, you can't believe

you're safe and picture splinters of all that glass
blasting in when wind
       comes off the lake like a hatchet.

In the carousel of the city, birds of paradise
thrust up from centerpieces
       like switchblades

while single file, the successful line up
for hand-carved slices
       of shoulder and butt, bleeding

under the warming bulb. They wag
their fingers, saying
                        Others are hungry,

so keep moving up, then they pass you
a toothpick
    in a crystal cup.

BLUE MANTILLA

When you picked up the hitchhiker
on the road to Red River though I said *No,*
and he sprawled across the backseat,

filled the car with a stink of sweat
and shit and talk of duct tape, then dug
through his triple-knotted knapsack

for *something awesome* to show us,
twenty miles of forest from anywhere
in New Mexico's wilderness,

I hissed *Stop the car,* but you hushed me
and smiled eagerly, as if we'd lucked
into some great adventure.

I didn't turn to look at the hollow book
he pulled from his sack or the *top secret items*
hidden there, but sat very still, curling

my fingers around the door handle,
and the plastic Virgin Mary glue-gunned
to the dash stared past me, her mantilla

spread like the boughs of blue spruce
standing mute under the sky, blank
and huge and empty for miles.

DAM

I painted your name on a dam
in Maryland, and now you owe me,
and I want everything.

I ruined my hands on the dam
then went home and slept a decade.
There's your name with paint on it—

and I slept with my face
on the grate. In Maryland,
men want to own

your paint. They make everything,
then name tall structures
after themselves. I painted you

a tall structure. Now the dam
is a ruin of wanting—you owe
my hands a decade.

Everything is on the grate.
Home knows your face, my sleep
is your ruined name.

BLACK APPENDIX

I.

My friend brings cheese and round crackers,
leaves them on the nightstand with a stub

of a knife. Far off, I hear her voice
muffled by the underbrush:

When you wake
we'll wash your hair and braid it.

All night I dream
of hunting mushrooms.

2.

The appendix I lost was black,
                                   short and blind.

It's in saline, bobbing—the bottle's called *specimen,*
                    the dark room's cold in Uptown.

They'll teach swirling it, saying, *Someone walked around*
                              too long with this, resisting.

3.

Maybe I've disappointed my dad
by drifting into disrepair, undermined
his care-taking.

Maybe I'm an old ship dragged from the harbor
and stuck in the soft earth
of a port town,

plugged with all manner of stuff:
garbage and gravel—it's called
cribbing the fill.

A city may grow over me with plaques
and statues and prayers shouted
on the street corners,

and if I should die,
I'd like to think of this:

myself as holding up,
myself as *crib*, filling.

4.

A nurse pulls
my glasses off,

tosses them.

Lying flat   is sharp.   We fly.

5.

Is this a cracker or a smashed life raft?

Is this singing or drinking through a straw?

Is this my mother or another sad tablet?

Is this a ship in a bottle or the devil's nasty tongue?

Is this a row of thick stitches or the tide at night ?

Is this a vein in my hand, or a glitter-star, burst apart?

6.

Leave my hair alone.

7.

I'm still pale with mushrooms,
still struggling
with fading.

Dark eyes in the center
of apples shame me,
so healthy.

But no one wants to hear
how my body
became a goblin,

how I watched it
chew me
into a pocked log

that fell into a ravine
of tall buildings:
mute, taking on water

until my friend hauled me
through Chicago
in a taxi—

wrapped in a long coat,
protesting,
dabbing on lipstick.

POEM ON THE ROAD TO DEPOSE

My body is a sack
of black spoons,
and my dreams
steal from me.

My books are full
of bite marks.

The lights outside Milwaukee falter—
good morning, corpse candles.

I've come zealously to represent
my client and will not listen

to the click
of the black spoons.

Purified by diesel
and the long gray bone
of the sky,

I am limb-caught and swallowed
by the monstrous laws of the dead.

LACE BLOUSE

Living never wore one out
so much as the effort not to live.
—Anais Nin

Because it cost too much,
and I couldn't arrange my face
in the way such delicacy demands,
I left the lace blouse in the vintage shop
and bought coffee, more books.

That night I dreamed
of birds at the ocean, even then
scolding myself: birds again—
senseless, short-lived, crying on the breakwater,
hiding their faces beneath flimsy wings.

GRATEFUL

After you hydroplane
into the guardrail,
you stand on the merge ramp
picking bits of mirror

from Queen Anne's Lace.
You wait for the authorities to come,
to determine your portion
of blame. But Fear arrives first—

solicitous in his big truck—
saying *We can hide this*
and rolling the accident
into the back, wrapping it

in a plastic sheet. Up front,
you sit folding your hands
quiet, grateful, dripping rain
all over the dashboard.

You try to ignore the water,
but Fear offers you an old towel,
snaps it   whip-like
at your face.

HURTS

I drove

        into the wrong rental car lot

and feared

        severe tire damage,

so I didn't back up

        to fix or apologize

but stayed

        stuck against the upholstery

all opened up

        like a puncture, like an ulcer

until I dried

        into an apricot: mute, solo,

a tough

        yellow tongue.

SISTER RIDDLE

I'm cutting hair. All night
shears flash
    in my hand.

I hold the tangles
for a moment but never
    bring them to my face,
never keep any.

I have so many sisters.
They pile up asleep
    on the floor.

I want to drop sugar water
in their mouths
    so they'll live 'til morning.

Instead, I light fires.

I see that bald, we look
nothing like
    each other.

I'll lose every one of them,
these pale animals
    dreaming of other
geography.

And they won't know me either,
just another
        tuft of hunger...

when we pass in the world,
we'll snarl.

FAILURE IN SMALL SPACES

Solace is holding

a cake of soap or a potato
in your hand,

saying *This is thick and basic,
and I need it.*

♦♦♦

 —except we were dancing
and dropped each other—

—except we held our own hands
in misery and prayer—

—and you woke at night
to eat the next day's food—

—and I burned the furniture
for the pop of varnish—

 —then we spit on the wood stove
and called it forgiveness—

that little spin and whiteness.

♦♦♦

Now our bodies are animals
in a wet cage, sleeping,

waiting for night to come,
for logs to hiss behind an iron door...

The stove reflects nothing,
but that's to be expected—

the stars are wooden,
our faces are in them.

THE TRAP

I bite my fingers viciously—
soon I'll eat away
                    the bull's-eye

of each print
and no longer be
                    a frantic raccoon.

Once free, I'll ease into camouflage,
a cool green kind
                    of nevermind.

But for now I sit around
with little red flags
                    of myself in my mouth.

DIGGING FOR BEETS

Everyone's kneeling

in the garden with implements—
thermometer, chilly speculum—

everyone's asking
how's the mulch and nitrogen…

Any day I'll begin

digging for beets—
turning the body habitable.

The cowbirds bark, *Yes*—
be something that's shaken
and dirt goes flying.

Beet. Starch.

From the cupola, I watch the earth.

It turns over. The windowsill
is a furrow of black flies.
I study them:

the split and brilliance
of still wings. Nothing

is like that lightness.

THREE

SLIP & FALL

To guard against it, the grocery stores
put plastic mats in the produce aisles
with holes the approximate size and shape
of the typical grape. I'm talking about liability.
I'm talking about avoiding the awful snap
of collar bone on linoleum, the shatter
of graham crackers and bifocal glasses.

I've been worried about the birds I cut
from construction paper that didn't look
like birds but anvils or trowels. Anyway
they did the job. Fewer bloody splotches
against the glass, fewer reasons to feel guilty
for getting in the way of hunger and abject
joy. I've been lost in the oil slick

of a junco's wing. I'm dark and sticky with it,
but regardless, all day I've been singing a poem
about traveling, singing even as I reach
for the phone to talk about insurance and risk
and plausible options, singing even though
everything I dream these nights is forests
and hands and bones and the winter rattles me.

It's a song about the end of caution—
an onyx pendant slipping from my neck
smashing on the supermarket's asphalt
where gulls are painted to ward off
a mess. But harm is not worth avoiding
if the cure is smallness... I wheel gladly beyond it
to the hole in the sky where birds are spiraling.

STOP

—after Tomaz Salamun

Stop.
Plot the dark and chisel it
across a cliff.

Then dance.

It's no longer there—
the dark—it dropped
like a musket ball.

It walked off.

It's missing in the alpine air,
the lichen, the bronchioles
of the big sequoia.

Now there's no telling.

The huge throat of the dark
is gone with all it swallowed:
eagles, ash fields, water,

the long tunnel of you.

STILL SLIPPING

She must not swing her arms as though they were dangling ropes,
she must not switch herself this way and that; she must not,
while wearing her bridal veil, smoke a cigarette.

—Emily Post

And I didn't. I was his curly headed sweetheart.
I carried peonies, a hanky, a special flower for his mother.
Thank you for making nice-nice, he said, but a month later

I'm still a length of string in a sloppy knot, still slipping
over the head of a catfish and dragging bottom. An alewife
bellows from the river bank—all outrageous wishes—

and when she sees there's no such thing as magic,
she's pissed—she uses me to strangle barnyard animals.
Oh dearest, call it an embrace. Call me a sash

in the prince's chamber holding back the drapes
so he can see from his bed. Out there, people are going
up in smoke—they're drifting over a hill

to a festival. Maybe it's a wedding—maybe
the smoldering is apple blossoms, and someone
is happy. Maybe this time the prince won't holler

his dead carp of best wishes from the window.
He'll be content to run the length of me through his hand,
and I'll obey. I'll switch this way and that.

On Wanting Only One Thing

for Patrick

This morning the hooded merganser
appears lazy on the lake, puckered feet tucked
beneath his rump so he's just coasting,
just carving with the cargo of his body

a sloppy channel through snake grass,
silent as a handbag. The merganser pays
no attention to kites swooping in the spruce,
loons keening in the coves or cormorants

airing their wings on the shore. The merganser
never swivels his head for sleep or grief
or even grooming, so it seems he might be stupid
or nearly dead. But then, at the bright twist

of fin beneath him, his soul becomes a syringe.
He unhinges his joints into sleek steel,
plunges through cold water, small heart soaring,
mind clenched behind hopeful, topaz eyes.

The Delight of Warehouses

We're good at dreaming ourselves
into abandoned places. We're best
at turning there, arms flung out,
saying *This isn't dancing,*
it's panicking. But it is dancing,
and others can't believe the smell

of concrete bewitches us into loving
basements, trestles, culverts.
Just as well. Their denial adds
to our delight of warehouses
and chicken farms where it's nice
to stand in front of dust-crusted fans
and sing a little. When we press

our mouths to the gallon jug
left all night on the prison steps,
we can scarcely keep ourselves
from gargling with happiness.
We brim with it, to think of it:
how the jug chokes up, gushes,
and how the dark becomes us.

THE FEAR CAT

The Fear Cat is dead with his lime eyes
and long claws, and I'm in a dark apartment

saying *The Fear Cat is dead...*
The Fear Cat is dead with his red paw

and longness, and now the air empties over me.

Without him is only.

The Fear Cat is dead with his legs stretched
and a blank face turned to what's left:

the apartment of too long,

the rooms of just warm enough.

The Fear Cat is dead, and now I walk out
in all this whiteness across a field of crows.

SPIDERS

This frayed red feather

with fleas,
with nothing

holding it in place
but a few fibers of flesh

is a fretful smile
flying drastically back

to the graying face
of my childhood house.

Waking up,

I smack against the window
and leave a kiss:

hasty and brick-like.

❖

You're the grackle—

glossy, resourceful, roosting
in this watchful town

and taunting God:
Turn up the wind!

hoping it's a turbine
pulling you toward danger,

requiring a brilliant display
of saving yourself.

❖

We're both saving receipts,
keeping every scrap that proves

we're trying. We're recording
our conversations, standing neck-deep

in cat-tails—tapping and barking
Testing... We left the city

for the ditch where we're sickened
by the sludge and bones and fur,

but oh it's worth it—we find hundreds
of bits of paper

and hug each other. At night fall,
we light a pile of brittle pods

and lean close to read the violet ink—
delicate, like spiders' legs.

❖

We say *Let's call the dog-catcher
on melancholy—*

this retching and whining
around the house each night

turn our days into deep suffering.
Babbling, we fall asleep

on staircases beneath tin-types
of ancestors and move too slowly,

like worms into the thick heart
of an elkhound.

❖

I've asked the cat-tails what they know. They deny
hunger, but anyone can see they're starving—

this autumn worse than ever—the sun bright
yellow apple and the nights thick as caramel.

They buckle their knees roadside, faint
with ugliness, and I remember a man marching past

not whistling, swinging a sharp edge. His wife
stayed up all winter hushing her children,

weaving bony stalks into baskets, fluffing pith
into quick-burning tinder.

❖

From the headboard, a face pointy and goat-like
laughs at me with its dark knot mouth, watching

out of whorls that wink in half-light. He wants
to kill me—he's walnut—the kind of tree that sets

the yard adrift in acid, so my dreams are all devils,
sulfur, and saplings curling like black tongues.

❖

If we leave each other, I'll blame
the taxidermist who stuffed an armadillo

and set it belly-up in his window—
a gray curved accordion gripping an old can

of Lone Star in its paws, its Pre-Cambrian tail stiff
as if with pleasure, giving us

the plastic eye of hopelessness.

❖

After days of rain,
we inspect the roof again
and find it's woven
in leg bones. There's no one

to blame. Spiders burrow in the marrow,
so we never see any lace-work
draped in the eaves. I talk too much
of being small and smoky here,

so tonight for something lovely

we rip off pieces of roof and start
a clumsy carving, fashioning
bones into rough flutes.

❖

In this house, the dead come up for air,
but by now I'm tired of ghosts and prefer
science: xylem and phloem, pulleys, siphons,
and when the kitchen smells of a sudden perfume,
or my husband speaks of blacksmithing in his sleep,
I sneak off to the shed where I've painted
the periodic table across one wall. I study it
until the cats drag past with a beaded purse.

❖

Blood-bellied spiders remind me
of beets pureed in a cold soup,
the tureen bending my face sideways,

and that's how I consider us:
coming out of a long curve between
shorn fields where crows stroll

in the mist. Spots of darkness,
that's all—small creatures, roots—
tucking into themselves for warmth.

The truck snorts in the cold. All the way
to town we're quiet and tired. You hold
my hair at the back of my neck like a nest.

Injury in Slumber

Let a candle burn throughout the night.
They will sleep in their robes, belted
but with no knives, thus preventing
injury in slumber.
—*The Rule of St. Benedict,* ch. 4 "How The Monks Are to Sleep"

A man builds prisons by day
and brings me vases of cosmos at dusk.

Once he washed my hair in a lake
and drank the water wrung from his fist.

Once he waited to dance with me
on cold tile and ate salt

and stood a fool in front of our fathers.
A man builds prisons.

I've made snow of our house and laid down
with vultures folded around me.

My pockets are full of bad words
and bus tokens, but all the while

his scent of sweat and pepper
has saved me. In this city,

he builds prisons then pulls gowns
through the mouth of a gargoyle.

The fabric is sleep, and I find him
at the stove in a dark kitchen

stirring a pan of bright stew.

I WILL NOT BE SAD IN THIS WORLD

after an Armenian melody

Though fog rolls
off the coast,

and a goat turns
its whiskey eye to find me
                and finds me...

I will not be sad in this world.

Though squirrels rise up laughing
even while begging
                forgiveness...

I will not be sad in this world.

Though my hands fill with whelks,
I build cairns, think in Braille,
                read flatness

in the ocean, and my soul dilates
like onyx. ...

I will not be sad in this world.

Not sad, not flesh filled with mist.

And not in this world,
though I crouch among spruce and ghosts
and kiss the mouth

I thought would be soft.

It is tight
                    with dirt.

The goat circles,
and I know...

but I will not be sad in this world.

ACKNOWLEDGMENTS

Grateful acknowledgment is made to the editors of the following
publications for first publishing these poems, a few in earlier versions:

Barrow Street: "Failure in Small Spaces"

The Cream City Review: "Spiders"

Epoch: "Dead Center"

The Florida Review: "The Peril of Gooseberries"

Forklift, Ohio: "Dam," "The Match Girl Lights Them One By One" and "Sleep"

Heliotrope: "The Physics of the Inevitable"

Mississippi Review: "Blue Mantilla," "Poem on the Road to Depose,"
"Red Brick Hungry," and "Slip & Fall"

New Millennium Writings: "On Wanting Only One Thing"

Oxford Magazine: "Digging for Beets"

Puerto del Sol: "Heat Rising"

River City: "Gold Stars" and "Lace Blouse"

Spillway: "Birds of Paradise"

The Spoon River Poetry Review: "Daughters," "Fine," and "Rolling"

Washington Square: "Stone Fruit"

"Still Slipping" appears in the anthology *Sad Little Breathings & Other Acts of Ventriloquism*,
published by PublishingOnline.

Special thanks to my parents for teaching me to love language and music and quiet, and to
Ellen Bryant Voigt and the Warren Wilson MFA Program community for creating a place of
such honest generosity. I am grateful for the support of my sisters and brothers: Judith,
Daniel, Maureen, Jennifer, and Paul, and of my friends: Matt Hart, Summer Heil, Joseph
Myer, and Mary Jane Nealon. Thanks also to my 5th grade English teacher, Emily Palfrey,
who encouraged my first poems.

I thank the Illinois Arts Council for the fellowship that helped me complete this book.